A GIRLS' ROAD TRIP:

FROM TEXAS (USA)

TO PRINCE EDWARD ISLAND (CANADA)

EULA WOODYARD MCKOWN

Olympus Story House

Table of Contents

Dedication

To my sister Julia Nation, and friends Vicki McKay and Len Roberson; without these three people, this trip would not have been the great experience it became.

A Special Thanks

to Wanda Sudbury, a wonderful friend who used her
expertise to edit my book.

Preface

My desire to travel began at an early age. After my mother taught herself to drive, she took us children with her when she visited her sisters. On one visit we went to see her sister who lived in East Texas, not far from the Texas border with Louisiana.

"We will drive across the border into Louisiana," my mother said as we left my aunt's house to return home. "Then I can say that I have been out of Texas."

My mother's action that day stayed with me after she passed away when I was 15 and planted the desire to travel in me. That desire was spurred on by one of my aunts who traveled to various places whenever she had the opportunity. Her sister-in-law lived in Arizona so that became one of her destinations at a time when a woman was not expected to travel that far by herself.

My twin sister, Julia, and I took the opportunity to visit our grandfather with our brothers while we were in high school. Upon graduation from high school, we found jobs in Houston, bought a car, and continued visiting relatives whenever we had the time.

After a year of working, we were given the opportunity to attend college. During the four years while we were completing our college education, we learned about more places and our desire to travel increased.

Graduating from college in 1965, we succeeded in getting teaching positions and began our careers as teachers. For the Thanksgiving holiday that year, my sister and I took our first road trip. A friend went with us to spend Thanksgiving with a college friend who had married that summer and was living in Nebraska.

At the end of our first year of teaching, we traveled to New Mexico to work for six weeks at Glorieta Baptist Assembly near Santa Fe. Following that job, we took our first major trip, traveling across the eastern United States. Our trip began in Nebraska where we again visited our college friend. From there, we traveled through Illinois to the east coast states, then traveled south, returning to Texas across the lower southern states.

The following summer, my sister and I took our aunt to visit her son and daughter-in-law in North Carolina. While there, we traveled to Washington, D. C. to see our nation's capital. When we left North Carolina to return home, we traveled south to Florida, then across the southern states, enjoying the Gulf of Mexico on our way home.

Those travels were the beginning of many vacations we have enjoyed. For all of those vacations, we planned where we wanted to visit, but we were flexible with our plans. We always traveled without reservations to stay in specific places, which allowed us to visit places of interest we discovered along the way and to find a place to spend the night whenever we were ready to stop.

When we planned our trip to Prince Edward Island, we continued our habit of being flexible and, for the most part, left where we spent the night up to how far we traveled during the day. Including two friends in our plans definitely added to the fun.

Introduction

My twin sister, Julia, and I began taking road trips together when we graduated from college and, over the years, we have taken many. Our road trips have been unique in many ways. The trips, like life, have been more about the journey than the destination.

In 2000, my sister Julia and I discussed traveling to Boston. When we discovered that our friend Vicki was to attend a conference in Boston in June, we invited her to travel with us and planned the trip around the dates she would attend the conference. To make the trip livelier, I also invited my friend Len to travel with us. All four of us had enjoyed the Anne of Green Gables stories and movies, so we chose Prince Edward Island (P.E.I.) as our farthest destination. The journey to P.E.I. would include whatever we chose to do along the way.

Since Julia and Vicki lived in Houston and Len and I lived 200 miles north, near McGregor, they came to my house where we began the journey. Because I had planned a Moody High School Student Council bake sale on Saturday, June 17th, we set that as our departure day.

CHAPTER 1

From Home to Kent, Ohio

June 17—I got up early to meet my students for the Student Council bake sale, which went so well that all of the food was sold by 9:00 A.M. After picking up Len, who lived just south of Moody, I returned home to finish packing for the trip so that Len and I would be ready to leave by the time Julia and Vicki arrived.

We traveled in Julia's van, a Dodge Grand Caravan. As large as it was, we still managed to fill it with our belongings. No one would believe the things we took on this trip! In fact, we had to decide what had to be left behind. We all had food to take; Len's was in a plastic tub. Because there was no room in the van for the tub, she took out the food she really wanted and left the rest behind. We were finally on the road by 2:30 P.M.

As was Julia's and my habit when traveling, most of the time we did not make advance reservations at places to stay, which made the journey more fun. However, I had made one reservation in Kentucky because our plan was to see the play about Stephen Foster, the songwriter, on June 18th; therefore, we knew we would be in Bardstown that night. Since Vicki was attending the conference in Boston, she had her reservation at the conference hotel. We had no other reservations; we could travel as slowly or as quickly as we desired. We could take time to sightsee, or we could forego seeing interesting things if time became a problem. With no reservations, we could travel long into the evening if we needed to go farther before stopping. Traveling without reservations provided the freedom of not having to stay within a certain schedule.

Traveling through Dallas and Texarkana, we arrived in North Little Rock before stopping to spend the night. We knew we needed to go as far as possible so that we could get to Bardstown, Kentucky the next day for the Stephen Foster play.

June 18—Continuing our trip, we traveled across Tennessee into Kentucky. However, we couldn't take time for sightseeing because we needed to be in Bardstown before late that night. We had reservations in Elizabethtown, but after Vicki checked the list of motels in Bardstown that I had printed from the Internet, we took her suggestion and cancelled that reservation so we could stay in My Old Kentucky Home Motel in Bardstown.

The motel was very nice and family owned, with the second generation of the family operating it. The play, *Stephen Foster The Musical*, was presented in an outdoor amphitheater and buses ran to area motels to pick up patrons. We didn't even have to drive to the theater; we rode the bus. We were advised that the bus would be best because if it rained, the play would move to the high school and the bus would take us there. Rain started to fall near the end of the first act, and we moved to the back of the theater to stand under the canopy. The rain stopped by the time the second act began, but we chose to stand under the canopy to watch the second act instead of going back to sit in wet seats.

The play was very good, and we learned that much of the story is based on what different people believe about Stephen Foster. Some do not believe that Stephen Foster even spent much time in Bardstown. He is remembered in Pittsburgh, Pennsylvania, where his family lived, in Bardstown, and in Florida.

June 19—The four of us toured Bardstown after locating the visitor's center and learning that a tour bus operated there. The tour bus was operated by America's largest family-owned distillery, the Heaven Hill Distillery, located in Bardstown, and a tour of the distillery was included; it was quite interesting; no samples, though, only a recipe book, Cooking with Bourbon. The only problem with that tour was that when I got off the bus, I didn't realize the top of the bus was so low, and I hit the top of my head on it so hard that walking quickly became a chore. I finally headed for the van because of my hurting head. Several Tylenol helped the headache, and by evening my head felt much better.

Len, Vicki, Julia, and Eula in front of bus

While I sat in the van, nursing my headache, Julia, Vicki and Len toured St. Joseph's Proto Cathedral in Bardstown. The architecture of the building attracted us to it. The cathedral was built in 1819, and is the oldest Catholic cathedral west of the Allegheny Mountains. When the three of them came back to the van, they were eagerly talking about the beautiful paintings they saw in the building, as well as describing all of the other interesting items in the church.

Upon leaving Bardstown, we drove southeast to visit the Shaker Village of Pleasant Hill, near Harrodsburg, Kentucky. Vicki had previously visited it, and she had been told that she really missed something by not trying the lemon pie. One goal, then, was to taste the lemon pie. We arrived in time for a late lunch in the Trustees' Office Inn, a place where everyone was dressed in period clothing and where the meals represented the Shaker meals. The meal began with a large bowl of coleslaw, followed by the entrees of our choice. The food was delicious, but we really didn't have room for lemon pie so we chose to purchase a whole pie to eat later. The pie was delicious, but we decided that the Inn was not accustomed to selling whole pies because the pie plate was a regular aluminum pie plate, not one that looked like it was to be sold. Julia kept the pie tin as a souvenir.

As we left the Shaker Village, we drove through Lexington, Kentucky to find our way back to the interstate highway. While traveling through town, in five o'clock traffic, we heard a crash behind us. Since I was riding in the back seat, I was able to turn around in time to see a car cross the traffic lanes to our left and bounce off the building that was near the street. Needless to say, we were ready to locate the interstate and leave the local traffic behind. When we arrived in Kent, Ohio, we stopped for the night.

By that time, Len had realized that she, a morning person, was traveling with three-night people. She was always ready to find a bed for the night long before we were. She would have stopped by 6:00 P.M. each evening if she had been allowed to make the decision. But since she was outnumbered three to one, we usually didn't stop until 9:00 or 10:00 P.M., sometimes even later.

CHAPTER 2

Kent, Ohio to Framingham, Massachusetts

June 20—Leaving the motel in Kent, we drove to Kent State University and toured the campus. Seeing the location of the riots that occurred there in 1970 was interesting. As we left the university, we were looking for the highway we needed when we saw a Land O' Lakes plant. Stopping, Julia and Vicki went in to see if we could tour the plant. Because the man who usually conducts tours was not there, we were not able take a tour, but, Julia and Vicki returned with souvenir Land O' Lakes cups. Len and I were somewhat disappointed that we didn't get one. However, I had plenty of that type of mug already.

As we drove across Pennsylvania, we looked for places of interest for sightseeing. The landscape was beautiful. Being in the northern area of the state, driving on Interstate 80, we knew that we had to get far enough east so we could reach Boston by the following evening. And, on the way, we had stops planned in New York and Connecticut.

I believe it was at one of our rest stops that day that Julia went into a convenience store while I stayed in the van, doing something. When she came out to the van, I was through so I went into the store.

"You must be sisters because I know she didn't have time to change clothes," the female clerk said as she looked at me. I laughed and explained to her that we were twins.

While looking at the road atlas, we saw Punxsutawney and decided to try to see Punxsutawney Phil, the groundhog. We exited the interstate and reached Brookville, Pennsylvania, a neat, small town just south of I-80. Because of nature's call, we decided to take a 15-minute stop in Brookville. The town was built on the slopes of the mountains and had some beautiful homes. The downtown area also had great architecture. Julia and I located a Ben Franklin store and became excited, not having seen one in years. Vicki and Len found us there and, of course, we had to do some shopping.

From the Ben Franklin store, we walked down the main street, visiting other stores. We met some very friendly people and enjoyed talking with all of them. While I was walking down a side street, I passed a young man.

"Hello, Ma'am," he said as he passed me, I was very surprised; I hadn't heard a young person speak so nicely in years.

Brookville was in the middle of celebrating the Laurel Festival, so we were able to learn more information about the buildings than was usually available. We went into one restaurant just to see the ceiling of the building, which was one of the oldest buildings in the town. Because that building was not included in their description of buildings to tour, I borrowed a menu from them, and had it copied so that we could have the description.

Our 15-minute visit in Brookville lasted three hours. When we left, we decided that it was too late to visit Punxsutawney Phil after all.

Driving along the interstate, we chose to see the twin covered bridges that were labeled in our atlas. Meanwhile, Vicki was reading some of her material on Pennsylvania and wanted to know what Pennsylvania Dutch cooking was. We had passed some billboards advertising the Dutch Pantry restaurants and were passing one when Vicki decided we should stop and see where more were located so that we could see the twin bridges and then eat at a Dutch Pantry restaurant. However, when Julia checked, we found that this restaurant was the last one going east; it was near Bloomsburg, Pennsylvania. We ate supper there. As we were leaving, Len mentioned that she taught school; the man working the cash register asked where.

"In Texas, near Temple..... near Waco," she said.

"My sister lives in McGregor," he replied.

"Who is your sister?" I asked.

"Jane S._," was his answer.

What a small world! I told him that Kimberlee, Jane's daughter, and my son Patrick are very good friends. He then went into the kitchen and got his sister Bonnie to come out and talk with us. Kimberlee had married in May, 1999, and I met Bonnie then. We had a good conversation with them, and I called Jane on my cell phone so that Bonnie and her brother could talk with her. That was an exciting surprise that added to our trip.

Although we spent extra time at the restaurant, we still managed to get to the twin covered bridges before dark. We took many pictures of the bridges; then we hoped it was bright enough for them to come out clearly.

Twin Covered Bridges: Julia in first bridge; Vicki and Len between the two bridges

As we traveled, we picked up some of the travel magazines that had discount coupons for motels. We began looking at them to see how far we could travel before finding a motel. We located a coupon for the Milford Motel in Milford, Pennsylvania, which was near the state line with New York. I called the motel and reserved a room for us, telling the clerk that we would be there at approximately 11:00 P.M.

The road construction near Wilkes-Barre slowed us down some. Then, just as we left Scranton, there was a dead deer in the road. Although Vicki, who was driving, tried to miss it, she ran over it with the left wheels of the van. A piece of the van's lower trim was pulled loose and we had to stop. A trucker who was driving behind us was very nice; he stopped and offered to help. He had tape and taped up the piece of trim, then told us about a truck stop across the interstate where we could get the underside of the van washed. He was kind and followed us to the truck stop to point out the area where the van could be washed to help get rid of the lingering odor from the deer.

By the time we left the truck stop, we knew it would be closer to midnight before we arrived in Milford. I called the motel and gave the lady an update on our arrival time.

"You will be in Room 20; I will leave the key under the mat," she replied.

When we arrived, the key was not under the mat; it was in the door! We were very glad to get into the room that night and had a good night's rest. Over all, though, our day had gone very well.

June 21—While everyone else got dressed and packed to leave, I dressed and went to the office of the motel where I checked us in and out, using the coupon from the travel magazine. We left the motel and drove around Milford, looking for a nice place for breakfast. When we didn't find an open restaurant, we turned around and drove through the town again. This time we got off the main highway and saw some nice old homes. A woman was working in front of her house, so we stopped and asked her about a restaurant. She was pleasant and told us that straight ahead was the Milford Diner & Restaurant, which had recently reopened and served good breakfasts. We headed to the location.

Once in the restaurant, we sat next to a couple that Len had seen at the motel. Some comments were made about staying at the motel. We found out that we had saved about $15.00 over their cost for the motel room by using the coupon. Then, as the couple left, the man stopped and asked if he could make an observation. When we agreed, he said, "I think blue and green are the same." We realized that he was referring to Julia and me being twins; she had on a green shirt and I had on a blue one. We received many similar comments about being twins throughout our trip. Although we didn't think we looked that much alike, many strangers did.

After finishing breakfast, we drove toward New York. Because we would be crossing the lower part of New York, we didn't have a great distance to travel before we reached the exit for Poughkeepsie. We were meeting Sue Roe and her son, Darrell, who were from McGregor, but were living in New York at that time. We met them at a Friendly's Restaurant and had ice cream.

Eula, Julia, Vicki, Sue, Darrell, and Len
at Friendly's Restaurant

While at Friendly's Restaurant, our group discussed attractions in the area and decided to tour the Vanderbilt mansion located at Hyde Park, New York. The mansion was built by Frederick William Vanderbilt, the grandson of Cornelius "Commodore" Vanderbilt, and Frederick's wife Louise. Louise enjoyed the lifestyle of the French royalty and their house was built to show that influence. We enjoyed the tour very much. To see the styles of homes the millionaires built before income tax came into existence was amazing!

Hyde Park, the Frederick Vanderbilt estate in New York

When our tour was finished, we left Sue and Darrell and continued driving toward Connecticut. Vicki had a friend from college, Cindy, who lived in West Haven, and we were to eat supper with her and her mother. Entering Connecticut, we spotted a Visitor's Center beside the highway. Agreeing that a rest stop was needed, we stopped. The Visitor's Center contained some interesting features. One wall had a mural which celebrated

P. T. Barnum's circus and there were a few cut-outs of characters where a person could put his/her face in a hole and have a picture taken, along with other displays. We thoroughly enjoyed taking that stop.

Mural of P. T. Barnum

As we continued to drive across Connecticut to reach New Haven, we savored the scenery. We were no longer on an interstate, and the highway followed the Housatanic River.

We arrived at Cindy's home in time for supper and were able to visit for a while. After supper, Cindy took us to see the boardwalk along Long Island Sound. As we walked the boardwalk, we saw Savin Rock, which was named for the Savin Trees that are on top of the Rock. During the American Revolution, the English landed on that area of the beach and marched into West Haven. The rock is also called "Old Abe" [Lincoln] or the "old sea captain" because the rock, if viewed in one direction, has the profile of a person's face.

Eula, Cindy, Vicki, and Julia on boardwalk

After we walked along the boardwalk and took pictures, Cindy guided us to the campus of Yale. We walked around it and saw the many buildings. Yale was so surrounded by the city that it didn't look like the universities we have in Texas. The visit was very interesting, but, alas, we had to leave because we had to make it to Boston before we could stop for the night. Vicki's convention had a trip to visit the L.L. Bean Order Fulfillment Center in Freeport, Maine on Thursday and Julia had signed herself, as well as Len and me, up for that trip.

Arriving in Framingham, a suburb of Boston, before midnight, Vicki thought that we should find a motel room first because she had her reservation at the Sheraton and a friend who was attending the convention was sharing the room with her. After stopping at one motel and finding that nothing suitable was available, we decided to find where the Sheraton was and see what was close to it. The Lord provides! Across the highway from the Sheraton was a Motel 6, and it had a vacancy. Julia, Len and I registered there for two nights so that we could sightsee in Boston before going on to Cape Cod.

CHAPTER 3

Sightseeing from Boston to Freeport, Maine and Back to Boston

June 22—Because we were so close to the Sheraton, it was easy for Julia, Len and I to arrive by 7 A.M. for the bus trip to the L.L. Bean Center. The bus was supposed to leave at 7:15 A.M. However, upon arrival we found that the bus was leaving at 7:30 instead of 7:15.

As we entered the bus, we found that we were supposed to have on closed-toed shoes. No one had provided that information ahead of time. Julia and I had on shoes which were almost closed, and Len's and Vicki's were fine. Some women managed to change their shoes, but others wore flip flops.

Our bus driver was very nice, and he made one stop for snacks before we reached Freeport, Maine. We managed to find souvenirs there, but decided to buy them when we traveled back through the area. We reached the L.L. Bean Center and had a most interesting tour. We learned how they filled the orders they received. One thing we noticed about the boxes was that most of the items were made in other countries, not in the U.S. Everything they had was computerized so that when a mistake was made, it could be tracked to the person who made the mistake.

After the tour at the L.L. Bean Center, our bus driver dropped us off in downtown Freeport to visit the L.L. Bean Factory Store and do other shopping. Freeport was known for its shopping district. The four of us and Liz, Vicki's friend at the conference, found a place for lunch; then we went our separate ways for shopping. Julia and I visited the L.L. Bean Factory Store and looked around for souvenirs. We both bought postcards and a book on lighthouses. When I checked out after Julia, the male clerk kept making remarks about what I bought. He guessed that I had 11 postcards, and I had the lighthouse book. Then, when I paid for the items, he commented on the $10.00 bill and change that I gave him. Finally, we realized that he had decided that Julia and I were twins, and he was comparing what she bought and how she paid for it with my purchases and payment method. We had bought the same things and gave him the same amount of money. He told me that he had a brother and sister who were twins and that they had a hard time adjusting when they went their separate ways. L.L. Bean also had a flagship retail store in Freeport that some members of the tour visited. However, Julia and I chose to not make that stop.

When we left Freeport, we traveled to Dover, New Hampshire, the home of McIntosh College. Our group visited the Atlantic Culinary Academy at McIntosh College and heard information about it. That was a most interesting presentation. McIntosh College was privately owned until the owner retired. Then a consortium purchased it. The Holiday Inn near the college was for sale, so the retired college owner purchased the motel and made arrangements with the college to use part of the motel for the Atlantic Culinary Academy. The Academy was sanctioned by Cordon Bleu of France, and the graduates received a Cordon Bleu certificate.

The Academy program was explained to us, and Vicki asked the chef how to cook an egg and flip it in the skillet. The chef demonstrated, and then had Vicki cook an egg and flip it. Vicki was thrilled when she was able to do it. She could brag to her sister, who taught Home Economics, that she could flip an egg, too.

Vicki learning to flip an egg

The Academy's building was not completed when we were there. The chef gave us a tour and explained what they expected to have in the near future. People from the area would be able to eat meals there, prepared by the students who were training to be chefs.

As we returned to Framingham, our driver said that we had time to take the coast route if everyone was willing to be a little later. We all agreed and he drove along the Atlantic coast, stopping at one location so that we could take pictures. We reached Framingham about 7:30 P.M. and were very willing to rest for the remainder of the evening, especially after we found out that the elevator was not working at the Motel 6, and our room was on the third floor!

June 23—When we checked out of the Motel 6, the elevator was still not working. The employees there learned how we travel. We had even taken the ice chest upstairs so that we could use it and replenish the ice. The manager helped carry our luggage downstairs and remarked that he felt like a pack mule by the time it was all down. I do believe that the next time the elevator breaks, they will try harder to have it repaired quickly.

Leaving Framingham, Julia, Len and I drove into Boston to sightsee. We had brochures on the trolleys we could ride around town and looked for a place to park so that we could catch one. We found a shopping center with a parking garage and a sign that said something about parking for $6.00. We decided to park in that garage because there was a trolley stop at the Marriott Hotel next door. We chose to ride the Old Town Trolley, which advertised "Sightseeing Boston's Best Tour." Never again! The ticket was good for only one complete trip. We could get on and off at the stops, but we missed stop #2 because our narrator failed to announce it. We got off at stop #3, the U.S.S. Constitution, and because the last trolley was at 4:30 P.M., we weren't able to get off at any more stops. Therefore, in essence, we had covered about half the tour.

The U.S.S. Constitution

At 4:30, when the last trolley was supposed to pick us up, it arrived full of people. The driver told us that another trolley was coming soon. We waited over 30 minutes and I finally tried to call about the trolley; I just got an automated message and was told to leave a message. There were approximately 30 people waiting for the trolley, but some of them were given a ride on a competing line. By the time the trolley arrived for us, over an hour late, there were about seven people left. The driver did cover the rest of the tour, minus the crossing into Cambridge.

When Len, Julia and I finally got back to the parking garage, we were thankful to see the van. However, when we left that garage, we learned a LOT about parking in Boston. The cost was $19.00 for the day. While we were at the U.S.S. Constitution, we saw a visitor's parking lot across from it that was free. We received an education about Boston that day.

The 'Big Dig'

As we left the garage, Julia, Len and I decided to do some touring of Boston on our own. Some of the streets were blocked because of the "Big Dig," which was a massive re-working of the streets in Boston. We saw large caverns which had been dug under streets and buildings. We drove through Beacon Hill (we had seen it from the trolley) and crossed the Longfellow Bridge into Cambridge. Unknowingly, we followed the route the trolley should have taken earlier. We drove through M.I.T. while there.

Leaving Cambridge, we somehow reached the exit for the tunnel to the airport. I wanted to travel through the tunnel so we went north. That was fine, but when we turned around and went south through the other tunnel, we had to pay a toll. We did make it out of Boston, though, and headed for Cape Cod, where we had a reservation at the Super 8 Motel in West Yarmouth. Because it was the weekend, I had made that reservation while in Boston to be sure we had a place to stay.

CHAPTER 4

From Boston to Cape Cod, Rhode Island, and New Hampshire

Along the highway to Cape Cod, we stopped for supper, found a nice family restaurant, and saw some interesting buildings. After reaching Cape Cod, we drove toward West Yarmouth and kept seeing signs that said, "Rotary Ahead." We could not imagine why such signs were on the highway. In Texas, the only "Rotary" we knew about was the Rotary Club. Finally, we reached the rotary—it was a traffic circle! We finally arrived in West Yarmouth around 9:00 P.M. and located our motel. Actually, it was almost in Hyannis.

The Rotary

Julia and Len had talked with two nurses while waiting for the trolley on Friday, and they had been to Newport, Rhode Island. They advised us to go see the homes there. As we settled in for the night, we checked our maps and made our plans for Saturday.

June 24—Departing our motel, Julia, Len and I drove into Hyannis to see the John Kennedy Museum. The museum was very interesting, and we learned more about the Kennedy family and the Kennedy compound.

Len and Julia at the John Kennedy Museum

Leaving there, we headed for Newport, Rhode Island. We stopped for lunch as we entered Rhode Island and saw a teacher from Connecticut. I asked her about teachers' salaries, and she said that their salaries averaged about

$77,000 a year. Of course, we were NOT thrilled to hear that, since the Texas average was about $35,000 a year.

In Newport, we found the visitors' center and received maps of the area so we could locate the mansions. We learned that Newport is located on an island; it is attached to the mainland only by a bridge. All of the mansions were built along the lower part of the city, along the coastline. We drove around to see them and then stopped to tour the Breakers, one of three mansions in Newport that were built by the Vanderbilts. The Breakers was built by Cornelius Vanderbilt II in 1895. The tour of the Breakers was especially interesting since we had toured the home built by Cornelius's brother Frederick in New York. The influence of the French could be seen here, also, and the view of the ocean from the Breakers was stunning.

The Breakers, the Vanderbilt mansion in Rhode Island

Leaving Newport, we chose to cross a bridge that goes onto the mainland of Rhode Island before driving back to Cape Cod. We just crossed the bridge, turned around, and drove back across it. Since Julia and I tend to take pictures of bridges that we cross, we enjoyed seeing the many different bridges as we traveled.

Reaching Cape Cod, we took the highway that we thought would take us to West Yarmouth. The highway did take us there, but it was the long way around! When we finally reached the motel, I checked the map. Julia, Len and I had seen most of Cape Cod by taking that road. We still managed to get to the beach and play in the water a little before it got too dark. Since we were staying in the middle of Cape Cod, and Julia wanted to drive all the way to Provincetown at the northeastern tip before we left, we agreed that we could do that if we left early the next morning. We made our plans.

June 25—Julia, Len and I got up and left around 8:30 A.M., heading east toward Provincetown. The drive was pleasant, and we saw many interesting areas. We even found a T-shirt shop where the shirts were 5 for $20.00. Considering that a bargain, we stopped and bought our souvenir T-shirts. We thought we would never reach Provincetown, but we finally did and took a different road as we headed out of town. The sand hills were very interesting.

As we were driving back, Julia realized that she had the motel room key in her pocket; she hadn't turned it in! She had discovered on the way to Provincetown that she left her large plastic cup at the motel, but we had decided to not retrieve it. Since the key was a regular key, though, we took it back and Julia found her cup. She was happy about that, but then we were late leaving to pick up Vicki, who was in Framingham, waiting for us.

Things progressed quite well until Julia, Len and I reached Boston. We took the interstate highway to reach the highway to Framingham. However, we misread the map and took the wrong direction. We ended up in Boston while looking for a way to get to the highway to Framingham. We found the street we needed; it just didn't go through the area where we were! Finally, we stopped, asked for directions, and drove to the highway. We found Vicki, loaded her things, and headed out of town.

As I drove, I realized that we needed to be going east instead of west. Julia looked at the map and said that we could go on west, so we did. We finally reached the outer loop and headed north. Since it was after 2:00 P.M., we looked for a place to eat lunch. We wanted a nice place because we were celebrating Julia's and my birthday, one day late. We had agreed to wait until Vicki was with us again to celebrate.

We found an exit with two restaurants and decided to check them out. We ate at the Ninety-Nine Restaurant & Pub in Hudson, Massachusetts. Because we wanted to go to Salem, I took the atlas into the restaurant so that we could see where we needed to go. One highway looked like the easiest way, so I asked the waitress where we were to pinpoint our location. After she told me, I asked how we could reach the highway.

"Take a right out of the parking lot, and that road goes to it," she replied,

The waitress was very nice and congenial. She asked Julia and me about being twins and said that her husband 'was' a twin. We had gotten information about the twin convention in Kent, Ohio, so Vicki asked if her husband would be attending the convention.

"I don't think so; he's six feet under!" the waitress replied, laughing. Vicki was embarrassed, but the waitress didn't seem to mind.

Upon leaving the restaurant, we followed the waitress's directions and found the highway to take us to I-95 so that we could visit Salem. Julia was in the front while I drove and Len and Vicki were in the back of the van. Suddenly, Julia and I began laughing so hard that we couldn't speak. Vicki and Len wanted to know what happened, but we still couldn't speak. Finally, I was able to tell them that we had passed a road sign which read, "Framingham 7 miles." We had traveled all that time and were then only seven miles from Framingham where we had picked up Vicki! As we continued on that highway, Julia was very pleased to see St. Julia's Catholic church. She wasn't too happy, though, when I didn't stop so that she could take a picture.

Because of all our 'travels' of the day, it was 5:00 P.M. when we reached the House of Seven Gables in Salem. Sadly, we couldn't go inside for a tour; it closed at 5:00 P.M. We did get to see the outside, and we saw other interesting places in Salem, including the Salem Witch Museum, before we continued on to Exeter, New Hampshire, where we would spend the night with Bud Young, Julia's and my cousin.

Bud had said that he wanted to take us out to eat. The four of us arrived at his home about 8:00 P.M. and he took us to Warren's Lobster House in Portland, Maine for supper. The food was delicious and we had a good time. Then, it was back to Bud's home so that we could sleep a while.

Julia, Vicki, Len, Bud, and Eula at Warren's Lobster House

Betty, Bud's wife, was visiting in Arizona, so Len and I slept in their bedroom, which was air-conditioned. The rest of the house had no A/C. Julia and Vicki slept on an air mattress in the living room and endured the warmth of the summer evening. Of course, people in the New England states are not accustomed to air-conditioning because they have so few warm days during the summer.

CHAPTER 5

New Hampshire to Prince Edward Island

June 26—Len and I took our dirty laundry to wash, so Vicki had an opportunity to sleep in the bedroom for a while. Then, it was time for us to continue our journey to reach Canada. Bud had wanted to take us sightseeing, but our escapades the day before had taken the time we had planned for it. However, as we left Exeter, we did drive through the town to see the lovely buildings and take some pictures.

Traveling through Maine, we decided to do some sightseeing in Kennebunkport and see the Bush Compound. We traveled along the coast and saw some beautiful sights, but nothing about the home of the former president. We went into town and found the visitors' center. Julia went in to get directions and maps. While she was there, I went into the liquor store next door to ask about recycling cans and bottles. I was told that they would take them if they were clean and rinsed. Consequently, we sat on the parking lot and rinsed the plastic bottles and aluminum cans we had in order to cash them in. We were paid 5 cents for each one. When you have to pay a deposit on them, you think more about returning them for recycling.

Julia came from the visitors' center with maps and verbal directions for us to reach the Bush Compound. She was told that there would be a place where we could pull off the road and see the compound; as we drove along the coast, we watched for that. When we found the location, other people were there. We got out to look and take pictures, and I heard one man tell another one that he was there because he had been to a teacher's conference in Boston.

"Which conference?" I asked.

He said that actually his wife had attended the conference and it was the marketing conference. I turned to Vicki and told her that his wife had attended the same conference she had.

"Well, hello, Eileen!" Vicki said as she looked at his wife.

His wife Eileen was the marketing teacher at Crosby, Texas, which is located near Humble (Julia's home) and Channelview (Vicki's home). Vicki knew her but had not seen her at the conference. We definitely live in a small world.

View of the Bush Compound from the highway

After visiting and taking pictures of the Bush Compound, barely visible across the water from us, we continued on our way to achieve our goal of reaching Canada that night. After checking the atlas, we decided to leave the interstate at Lincoln, Maine and travel into New Brunswick, Canada, which would save several hours. The highway was only a two-lane road through small towns and across mountains. Len was not thrilled with some of the turns, but we did enjoy the ride. We were hoping to see a moose or two, but none ever appeared.

By the time we finally reached the border crossing, the clock in the van had 11:33 P.M. We stopped on the U.S.A. side and talked with the agent. He asked all sorts of questions, and we answered them. He asked if we had seen any moose and we told him that we hadn't. He said that the vehicle which had been ahead of us had seen about four.

"You know you lose an hour when you cross the river," he continued.

We hadn't realized that, but the St. Croix River between the U.S. and Canada border stations was the time zone line, so it was about 12:45 A.M. when we reached the Canadian station.

The St. Croix River between the U.S.A. and Canada

While at the Canadian station, we asked about the next town and was told that McAdam was about 10 kilometers away. (We had to adjust to using metric!) We asked if a motel was located there and were told that there was one and that there was a sign on the office door with a phone number to call to rent a room. Also, a phone booth would be there to use. We then continued on to McAdam.

We reached the 'big' city about 1:00 A.M.; its population was under 2,000. Finding the motel and the phone number, I tried the phone in the booth, but it did not work. We drove back down the street to see if we could find another phone booth. As we passed a home, we could see that a man and woman were sitting at their dining table. He watched us as we drove by the house.

When we didn't find a phone, we turned around to go back toward the motel. As we approached the same house, the man was standing outside and motioned for us to stop. He asked if we needed help. We told him that we were looking for a phone to call for a room. He told us to get out and come into his house; we could use his phone. I got out and started into the house when he told me to tell the others to get out, also. I did, and as Julia, Vicki and Len were getting out of the van, a car stopped in the middle of the street and the man driving asked if we were trying to rent a room at the motel. When we said yes, he told us that he would go get the man; and he turned around and left. I told John, the man who had stopped us, that we didn't need to use the phone and that the other man was going to get someone for us. He insisted that we go into his home anyway, so all four of us went inside.

John introduced us to his wife, Carla, who was working at the table. They explained that they had just come from Lincoln, Maine; they were the ones who had seen the four moose ahead of us. We visited with them until someone called and told John that we could go to Klinger's Lounge and that someone would be there to rent us a room. We thanked John and Carla for their help and went to the lounge. Because each room had only one double bed, we had to rent two rooms, but we were thankful for a place to spend the rest of the night.

Klinger's Motel

June 27—Annie's Restaurant was between Klinger's Lounge and Klinger's Motel. We began our day by eating breakfast there. Julia, Len, and Vicki went with the traditional breakfast items, but porridge was on the menu so I chose to order it. It turned out to be oatmeal, but our waitress wrote it on the check as 'otmeil.' We had a laugh over that.

After paying for our meals with American money and watching the problems of converting it, we decided to go the bank and convert some of our money so that we would be prepared to pay with Canadian funds. Also, McAdam had a beautiful railroad station and we wanted to see it before we left town.

McAdam was a nice place with very friendly people. The city was preparing for their "Celebration 2000" the next weekend and we found some good buys on souvenirs at the local drugstore. The railroad station had been built 100 years before, and they were preparing to celebrate it. The station was no longer in operation, but it had two stories, and the Canadian Pacific Railway once operated a first class, five-star hotel there. The station had also contained a lunch counter, dining room, offices, baggage/freight facilities, and even a jail. For a small town, McAdam had a number of historical buildings, including its post office and library.

The historic railroad station in McAdam, New Brunswick

Finally leaving McAdam, we made our way toward Prince Edward Island, our Canadian destination. There were two ways to reach the island—bridge and ferry. Because people didn't pay to go to the island, only to leave, and the ferry cost more than the bridge, we decided to go to the island by ferry and leave by bridge. We picked the shortest route we could find, but of course, we had to stop and sightsee. The countryside was beautiful and the land was not nearly as populated as in the United States. Even buying gasoline was interesting because it was priced by the liter instead of by the gallon. The cost looked much lower, but it took a lot of liters to fill the van's gas tank.

We drove through Fredericton, the capital of New Brunswick, and on toward the ferry. For quite a while we followed a body of water, which was the St. John River and Grand Lake. At one point, I saw a sign for a ferry that crossed the river to Gagetown. We didn't check out the ferry, though; we continued on toward P.E.I. By the time we reached Moncton, our group decided that we would not make it to the ferry crossing on Nova Scotia before the last ferry left, so we decided to take the bridge to P.E.I. and to come back by way of the ferry.

When we reached Sackville, we saw a visitors' information center and stopped. The building was unusual; it was octagon shaped and had been a home at one time. While in the center, we learned about a covered bridge near there and asked for directions to it. We learned that we could drive out to see the bridge, cross it, and continue on to the highway we needed to reach P.E.I. We then left for another adventure.

Vicki, Eula, Julia, and Len at Sackville Visitors' Center

On our way to see the covered bridge, we saw a beautiful church. When we stopped to take pictures of it, we learned that it was the oldest Baptist church in Canada. We found the covered bridge, took pictures, crossed it, and continued on our way to P.E.I.

Middle Sackville United Baptist Church
Founded 1763—Oldest Baptist Church in Canada

Covered bridge near Sackville, New Brunswick

We reached the Confederation Bridge early enough to take pictures before we crossed. The bridge was ten miles long and had enough curve in it to keep a driver awake. It was a two-lane bridge, so there was no passing on it. [The bridge had been open for only ten years; before then, the only way to reach the island was by ferry.]

Confederation Bridge

CHAPTER 6

Touring Prince Edward Island

When we exited Confederation Bridge on the P.E.I. side, we were at Gateway Village, an area of service stations and businesses for people to shop and eat. We stopped there and Julia asked about a place to spend the night. Julia was advised that if we continued down a certain highway, we would find some inexpensive motels before we reached Summerside. She was also told that a very nice restaurant, Brothers Two, was located in the city. Again, we left in search of a room for the night.

We saw the Mid Isle Motel & Coffee Shop, but we did not realize that it was in Central Bedeque, not near Summerside. We liked the looks of the motel and rented a room while one was available. Then, we realized that it wasn't air-conditioned! Thankfully, there were screens on the door and windows. They kept out most of the mosquitoes, which were huge; larger even the ones we had in Texas.

After putting our things in the room, we left in search of the Brothers Two restaurant. Everyone had said that it was a good restaurant. We found Summerside where it was supposed to be, but we didn't find the restaurant. Finally stopping for help, we were given more directions. As we drove to the restaurant, we realized that we had not been on the main street of the town. After getting on the main street, we saw many more businesses on our way to the restaurant.

Brothers Two was a good place to eat and we really enjoyed it. Our waitress was very friendly and told us a lot about the area. There were brochures advertising a dinner-theater so we asked about it. The waitress explained that if we had been there at 6:30 P.M., we could have eaten and enjoyed the dinner-theater. The actors in the theater were also the waiters and waitresses for the meal. The meal was served between the acts of the play. We decided that on our next trip, we would get to the restaurant early enough to see the play.

Next door to the restaurant was a motel. Our waitress explained that it was owned by the same family that owned the restaurant. During the winter, when the weather was so bad the employees couldn't travel home, they were given a place to stay at the motel. She told us about one night when she was not able to get home and had returned to the restaurant to stay at the motel.

After eating, we returned to our motel to prepare for seeing Prince Edward Island the following day. We made note of the highway sign that directed us to the first school where Lucy Maud Montgomery, the author of the Anne of Green Gables stories, had taught. We planned to see it the next morning.

June 28—When Julia, Vicki, Len, and I left the motel, we drove toward Summerside to do some sightseeing. On the way to the one room school house where Lucy Maud Montgomery had taught, we visited a fabric store which we had seen advertised on a billboard on the highway. There I got directions to the school, and we found it, but it was not open. We were disappointed that we didn't get to see inside, but we could look through the windows.

Lower Bedeque School where Lucy Maud Montgomery taught

Departing from the school, we traveled on to Cavendish to see the area made famous by Lucy Maud Montgomery's books about Anne of Green Gables. Upon reaching New London, we saw a sign for the house where Lucy Maud Montgomery was born and stopped to tour it. Homes were really small in the 1800s.

Birthplace of Lucy Maud Montgomery

While waiting on Len and Vicki to finish shopping at the souvenir store across the street, Julia and I went to the gas station next door. I was surprised to find that they had bottles of Dr Pepper. I asked if they had Diet Dr Pepper. The people said they had never heard of it. I told them about the different types of Dr Pepper we could buy at home and they were very surprised; all they had was regular Dr Pepper. I bought a bottle of it, drank it, and saved the half-liter bottle as a souvenir.

Journeying on to Cavendish, we stopped for lunch at a nearby restaurant. We asked about locating a bank, and our waiter told us that the nearest one was many miles away. He explained that the population of Cavendish during the winter was only about 40 people, so there was not much located there. He directed us to a strip of businesses so that we could buy souvenirs. Most of the places were open only during tourist season. Later, we learned that tourist season didn't really begin until July 1st. We were glad to be there before the influx of thousands of people.

When we ordered our meal, we also ordered tea. Vicki asked for Sweet and Low for her tea, and the waiter brought some sweetener. After putting the sweetener in her tea, she tasted it and said, "The tea is already sweet."

When the waiter returned, she asked him about the tea, and he said that they always serve sweet tea; no one asks for unsweetened tea. Vicki told him that he might mention that to people when they order tea. We learned not to sweeten our refills.

As we drove on toward the House of Green Gables, we noticed a village for Avonlea, an area similar to a theme park. We drove through it, but decided it was not our destination. The village looked like it was in the process of being built; the buildings imitated the story of Anne of Green Gables: the house, church, train station, etc.

The House of Green Gables is part of the Prince Edward Island National Park in Canada. We could purchase tickets with American money because the registers at the ticket booths are programmed to automatically give the current rate of exchange. I purchased my ticket with $50.00 in American money. The rate of exchange was so broad that I received my ticket and almost $75.00 in Canadian money for change.

The House of Green Gables had belonged to the aunt and uncle of Lucy Maud Montgomery and was believed to be the setting she used for her Anne of Green Gables stories. The rooms in the house were decorated to represent the rooms described in the Green Gables books. The bedrooms upstairs were for Marilla and Anne. Because of Matthew's heart condition, he could not climb the stairs. His bedroom was downstairs, between the dining room and kitchen. In the movie, Anne of Green Gables, Matthew told Anne that he hadn't been upstairs in two years.

"I see why Matthew didn't come upstairs. These stairs are too narrow and steep," stated Vicki as we climbed the stairs.

House of Green Gables

Because of the limited number of tourists, we were able to leisurely tour the house. We took our time looking at each room and were able to take plenty of pictures. We were told that after July 1st, only 20 tourists would be allowed in the house at one time. Once again, we were thankful to be there before the official tourist season began.

A barn on the property represented how the people provided for themselves. A small theater inside the barn showed videos to help visitors learn more about Lucy Maud Montgomery. Len, Julia, and I watched one together. By the time the video was finished, Julia was so sound asleep that she didn't know it ended. She was upset when Len woke her because then the other people in the theater also knew that she had been asleep. (Julia had told us that she would probably go to sleep and for us not to bother her.)

Also, in front of the house was a trail through the woods that people could follow to see the area Lucy Maud Montgomery wrote about in her books. Vicki and Julia walked down the trail and into the woods, but I decided to save my energy. There were too many steps to walk down and then back up and my knees didn't feel like tackling them. Of course, there was a souvenir shop for us to visit before we left.

Trail into the woods at the Green Gables Heritage Place

Leaving the park, we drove through town where we saw the post office and stopped to mail some things. We had read and heard that Lucy Maud Montgomery's grandfather was postmaster and that they lived in the post office. The house her grandparents lived in had burned, but a house similar to it was purchased and moved to the town to become the post office. A display area inside the post office showed what the post office was like when Lucy Maud Montgomery's grandfather ran it. A life-sized poster of Lucy Maud Montgomery welcomed visitors to the post office.

Julia with the Lucy Maud Montgomery poster

Leaving the town, we drove on along the northern coast of Prince Edward Island with the goal of riding the ferry to Nova Scotia as we left Canada. Vicki said that she still had not waded in the waters on a beach so, as we got closer to Wood Island to catch the ferry, Julia and I noticed a beach with steps leading down to it. There was also a park area with a volleyball net. Julia thought it was a private residence, but as we passed it, we saw a public park sign. I turned around, and we went back so Vicki could see a beach. We all took off our shoes and played in the water. The water was so clear we could see everything on the bottom of the ocean there. It was very pretty and we enjoyed the stop. We also found pine cones that we picked up and added to our collection that we had begun earlier on the trip.

Vicki wading in the water

Soon we decided that we had better leave so we could reach the ferry. We continued on without any problems and followed the signs to Wood Island. As we drove up to the toll booth for the ferry, we saw the ferry at the dock.

"You just missed the last ferry," the woman in the booth said as we sat there watching the ferry leave the port.

Since we didn't have time to spend the night and catch the ferry the next morning, we turned around and drove toward Confederation Bridge. Missing the ferry also meant that we missed visiting in Nova Scotia, another place to visit if we made the trip again.

CHAPTER 7

Prince Edward Island to Maine

Julia, Len, Vicki, and I retraced our route and determined the closest way to reach the Confederation Bridge. Vicki knew by this time that her mother was not expected to live very long, so we wanted to make as much time as possible. We crossed Confederation Bridge in time to see the sunset and continued on to Moncton, where we searched for a motel room for the night.

As we entered the city, we stopped at one motel and I went in to ask about a room. The rate was higher than we wanted to pay, and the woman was not very friendly. Although she said that we probably would not find another room in town, we decided to risk it and headed back to the highway.

We drove to another exit for the town and began to travel down what appeared to be a main street. We saw the Elmwood Motel and stopped. Yes, a room was available, and the rate was reasonable; therefore, we spent the night there. I had asked for a room on the ground floor and it was; it just had about 14 steps up to it. It was a spacious room, and there was an ice machine where we could get plenty of ice to replenish the ice chest. We slept so comfortably that we didn't hear any of the noise that supposedly went on outside during the wee hours of the morning.

June 29—We left Moncton, New Brunswick with plans to reach Vermont so that we could do some sightseeing there before heading on home. As we traveled across New Brunswick, headed toward McAdam, we again reached the area of Grand Lake. I saw a sign that said the ferry was operating. When we reached the ferry crossing, I turned into it. The ferry was coming toward our side with one pickup truck on it. It docked, the pickup drove off, and I drove onto the ferry. Before we knew it, we were going across the lake. There were no fees and we never saw a person. We reached the other side, drove through Gagetown, and again made our way to Fredericton, which was on our way to McAdam.

We reached McAdam before noon and Julia said that she wanted to try a lobster roll. Mae's Place, a café in McAdam, advertised lobster rolls, so we stopped to try one. As we entered the small café, Julia asked the price of the lobster roll. She was told that it cost $6.99. She asked why the roll was so expensive. The owner explained to her that it had a lot of lobster in it. By then I was laughing because I realized that Julia was talking about a bread roll and the owner was talking about a type of sandwich. The owner explained that the lobster roll was lobster in a hot dog bun. Julia, Len, and I ordered one and found out what a hot dog bun in Canada was like. It was about the size of ours, but it looked like a thick slice of bread that had been sliced almost through the middle. Because it was flat on each side, the bread was toasted to be used for lobster rolls. It was good, but I don't know that I'll ever eat another one. We did a little more sightseeing in McAdam before we headed for 'the States.'

Upon reaching the border stations, we checked with the Canadian station for clearance so that we could leave Canada.

A little later, while we were at the U. S. station, we realized that we needed information about what to do if we wanted to try to obtain a refund of the Canadian tax we had paid. Therefore, after clearing with the U. S. station, Julia drove back to the Canadian station for information.

Julia parked under the awning behind the Canadian station and went inside for details while Vicki went inside to use the restroom. Len and I stayed in the van, Len in the back seat and I in the front passenger seat. When Vicki returned, she decided to stand outside the van while waiting for Julia. We heard tires squealing and looked up to see a pickup, which was towing a camper, rounding the curve of the road that led to the Canadian station. As we watched, we were not sure if the driver would maintain control of the pickup. If he didn't, he was headed straight toward us. Vicki went behind the van and Len and I couldn't move inside it. Inside the station, the attendant told Julia that someone else was about to wipe out their awning; that it had happened before. The driver managed to control the pickup enough to make the curve without hitting us. Then, Vicki realized that going behind the van was not a good idea. If we had been hit, the van would have been pushed into her. Len and I knew we should have gotten out of the van, but we were frozen for that moment. When Julia came out of the building, she realized that her van was parked under the awning that the attendant had said was about to be wiped out. We thanked the Lord that the accident had not occurred and left for the good old U.S.A.

CHAPTER 8

Maine to Pennsylvania

As we traveled, we realized that we couldn't visit both Niagara Falls and Hershey, Pennsylvania, so we chose to go to Hershey. However, we had stops planned in Vermont first. As we crossed Maine, we continued to hope to see a moose, but the only ones we found were carved ones. We did like the 'watch for moose' signs we saw on the highway. There were several types of highway signs in that part of the U.S. that one won't see in the south.

One wooden moose

Our first destination in Vermont was Stowe, where the von Trapp family of "Sound of Music" fame had settled. We reached Stowe after dark, and it was difficult to see anything. I stopped at a gas station to ask about a motel (later, I found out that the gas station was at the only intersection in the town). I was told that there were some inexpensive ones down a different highway than the one on which we had entered, so we headed to them. We located two, owned by the same family, and I checked on the price of a room. It was over $100, so we decided to go to a motel ten miles away that we had located while at the gas station.

While in the gas station, I had picked up a tourist map and Vicki was looking at it. She noticed an ad for The Riverside Inn in Stowe, and we decided to check it out. It was very close to the other two that were supposed to be inexpensive. We found the inn and I asked about a room. Yes, they had one and yes, it was inexpensive. The room was large and had two double beds and a single bed for our use. There was also a coffee pot, which many of our earlier motels didn't have.

The owner brought us a tray with the coffee 'fixings,' including china cups and saucers. We were impressed.

The Riverside Inn was located on the banks of a small river. There were picnic tables along the river bank where guests could picnic during their stay. Unfortunately, we did not have time to enjoy that area.

June 30—The owner of the inn was outside as we were getting ready to leave. Because of his accent, we asked where he was from. He told us that he had lived north of London, but came to the U.S. and enjoyed it so much, he decided to stay. His family bought The Riverside Inn in 1997.

Our plans were to eat breakfast at the Trapp Family Lodge, so we asked directions and left. The lodge was up in the mountains, and the area was beautiful. While enjoying our breakfast at the inn, we were given some information about the family.

Eula, Vicki, Julia, and Len enjoyed breakfast at the
Trapp Family Inn

Maria, one of the von Trapp daughters, was still alive and had a room in the lodge where she stayed whenever she decided to visit there. We were told that there were photographs and a family tree in the lodge and that we should see them. After breakfast, we walked through the lodge in search of those things. Then we went to the souvenir shop to purchase our mementos of the von Trapp family. The van had been filled long ago, but we continued to buy.

Even though it rained that morning, we enjoyed seeing the Trapp Family Lodge and the scenic view of the land around it. When we left, we drove to the Ben and Jerry's ice cream plant and took its tour. The plant was interesting, and we did get samples of ice cream at the end. Of course, there were more souvenirs to purchase.

We traveled on toward Burlington, Vermont to see the Dakin Farms store. Vicki wanted to visit it and the Teddy Bear Factory, which was farther south. When I checked the tourist map (Vermont has great tourist maps), the store was right at the exit we were taking for Burlington, so it would be easy to visit. We weren't sure about the Teddy Bear Factory, though. Also, when I checked the atlas, I saw that we needed to cross Lake Champlain in the area of Burlington so that we could reach the interstate in New York to head south. By this time, we knew that Vicki's mother was critical and we needed to head home as quickly as possible. At a visitors' center, I found some brochures about the ferries that crossed Lake Champlain. We could cross in Burlington, or drive south in Vermont to Charlotte and cross on the ferry there. The crossing at Charlotte was much shorter than the one at Burlington, so we decided to make the crossing at Charlotte.

When we exited for Burlington, we made our stop at the Dakin Farm Store. The displays were interesting, especially the one which showed a maple tree with the bucket to illustrate how the sap was collected to make maple syrup. We left the store with several purchases, including bottles of real maple syrup.

Eula at the maple tree exhibit

As we drove through Burlington in search for the highway to Charlotte, we noticed Lake Champlain in the distance and decided to drive on to see it. We passed a building and wanted pictures of it, so I got out and took pictures while Julia, Vicki and Len drove around the block. Then we went to the end of the street to see the building that had attracted our attention. Lake Champlain was right behind it.

The building turned out to be Union Station, the former home of their railroad. Vicki and I took pictures, and I went inside the building to explore more. Various businesses were located inside the old train station. I asked at one window if the trains still ran. I was told that they did not, but a commuter train was to begin operation between Burlington and Charlotte in October. When I returned to the van, I asked the others how many ways they could pronounce "Charlotte". On Prince Edward Island, everyone said "Charl-ton," for Charlottetown, and the lady in Union Station had said "Char-LOTTE."

Driving to find the highway to Charlotte, we stopped at a red light. At the curb was a man on some funny-looking strips with wheels. We finally decided that he was training for cross-country skiing. When the light changed and he took off down the street, we knew we were correct. He had poles to push himself off, and he used skiing motions as he traveled quickly down the street. We wanted a picture, but I wasn't fast enough with the camera.

We finally found the road to Charlotte and continued our drive through Burlington. We stopped at a gas station, and a fellow customer asked what we were doing in Vermont. We told him that we were vacationing. He was also told about the deer we hit in Pennsylvania. He told us there were so many deer in Pennsylvania that during deer season, the hunters stopped on the side of the interstate highways to shoot deer and that it was legal. We didn't want to be in Pennsylvania during deer season.

While traveling toward Charlotte, I checked the tourist map again and saw that the Teddy Bear Factory was right on the way, so we were able to stop there. We were too late to take a tour of the factory, but we did watch a bear being stuffed. After stuffing the bear, the employees allowed the child who would own the bear to 'cut the umbilical cord', the plastic thread at the end of the last stitch. Then they announced the date and time of the 'birth' of the bear and gave the child a birth certificate. Of course, we couldn't pass up their visitors' center to look for more souvenirs.

Vicki, Eula, Julia, and Len at the Teddy Bear Factory

Leaving the Teddy Bear Factory, we continued to Charlotte to locate the ferry. The highway to the ferry was interesting. The area was very rural, and we didn't think we would find a ferry at all, but we did locate the crossing and did not have a long wait. Since we were first in line, we knew we would make it onto the boat. The lake was very pretty, and we enjoyed our crossing. We had gotten our ferry ride after all.

Vicki, Len, Eula, and Julia enjoying the ride on the ferry

The exit on the New York side was in just as rural an area as the road to the ferry in Vermont had been. Julia was driving, and we were watching highway signs and looking at the map, but we still began to think that we had missed the road to the interstate highway. Just when we were sure we were not where we should be, we saw a sign to the interstate. We found it and drove south.

As we got closer to Albany, we realized that if we followed the interstate, we would be going back east and we needed to go west to connect with Interstate 88, which ended at Schenectady, New York. Therefore, at Saratoga Springs we exited for Highway 50 and headed toward Schenectady. Of course, we saw places along the way to stop and take pictures. In Ballston Spa we found some beautiful churches where we took pictures and continued on our way.

Late in the day we entered one town near Schenectady and saw a lot of people walking around. As we drove on, we saw even more people. When we got to the main highway through the town, there were people everywhere. They were sitting beside the highway, and the traffic was so heavy that the police were directing traffic. We were stopped in line at a red light, and it seemed that the cross traffic was the only traffic being allowed to go. Julia rolled down her window and asked a man what was going on. He said that they were getting ready for fireworks; we might as well park and watch them, because the traffic was so bad that we wouldn't get out any time soon. Before long, though, the police motioned for our lane of traffic to go, and we left the offer to watch fireworks behind. We found our way to I-88 and headed southwest.

We reached Binghamton before stopping for the night. We found a Super 8 Motel just off the interstate and chose to spend the night there. By this time Vicki knew that her mother might not live until we got back to Texas so our goal became to drive as quickly as possible to Texas. We gave up the plan to visit Hershey, Pennsylvania.

NOTE: Before we left on vacation, Vicki had visited her mother and said her goodbyes. Vicki had planned to attend her conference in Boston and knew of the possibility that her mother would pass away before she returned home.

CHAPTER 9

Pennsylvania to Texas (Home!)

July 1—We left Binghamton and crossed Pennsylvania into Maryland. We really liked the roadside signs in Maryland—they warned us to watch for moose and bears. We wanted a picture of it, but didn't manage to get one. From Maryland, we crossed West Virginia, Kentucky, and made it to Fairview, Tennessee before stopping for the night. Actually, we tried to find a room on the west side of Nashville, but the motels were full. We were told that we could probably find one a few miles down the road. When we saw the sign for the Dickson Motel, we stopped. That motel had not only our least expensive room for the entire trip, but also our largest. Even with three double beds in the room, we had plenty of room to move around. Also, the room was air-conditioned.

The next morning Julia talked with the owner of The Dickson Motel and found out that he had owned it for only three months. We then understood why the swimming pool was not cleaned and other things needed to be done. The owner had enlarged the lobby and offered a continental breakfast for the guests, so the motel was not bad at all.

July 2—Julia, Len, Vicki, and I took advantage of the continental breakfast and continued on our journey to Texas. When we stopped at a truck stop about 10:30 A.M., Vicki called home. She found out that her mother had just died. We knew we had to get to Dallas today.

As we crossed Arkansas, Vicki saw an exit for Stuttgart. She asked if we minded going through Stuttgart because that was where her mother had lived for many years. Of course, we didn't mind. We exited and drove south to the city. The drive was very nice and the farming area was pretty. We located the First Baptist Church where her mother had attended church, and Vicki took pictures. She then picked a rose to take for her mother's funeral. As we left town, she also picked some wildflowers.

We had no difficulty going from Stuttgart to Pine Bluff, Arkansas and on to Malvern where we picked up the interstate again. We drove on to Texas, and reached Vicki's mother's house in Dallas about 8:00 P.M. Vicki's family was there, waiting for her to arrive. After seeing Vicki's family, Julia, Len and I continued toward home. We took Len home first, so Julia and I arrived at my home around 11:00 P.M. Our last day had been long, but we truly enjoyed the trip that had taken us all the way to Prince Edward Island in Canada and brought us safely home again.

Motels:

The motels where we stayed on this trip provided lasting memories for us. I have included the list of them so that other travelers may choose to visit one or more of them and make their own special memories.

June 17 — North Little Rock, Arkansas, U.S.

June 18 — Old Kentucky Home Motel, 414 W. Stephen Foster Avenue, Bardstown, KY 40004, U.S.

June 19 — Super 8 Motel, Kent, Ohio, U.S.

June 20 — Milford Motel, Milford, Pennsylvania, U.S.

June 21-22 — Motel 6, Framingham, Massachusetts, U.S.

June 23-24 — Super 8 Motel, West Yarmouth, Massachusetts, U.S.

June 25 — We spent the night in Exeter, New Hampshire, U.S. with Bud Young, the cousin of Julia and Eula

June 26 — Klinger's Motel, McAdam, New Brunswick, Canada

June 27 — Mid Isle Motel & Coffee Shop, Central Bedeque, Prince Edward Island, Canada

June 28 — Elmwood Motel, Moncton, New Brunswick, Canada

June 29 — The Riverside Inn, 1965 Mountain Rd., Stowe, Vermont 05672, U.S.

June 30 — Super 8 Motel, 771 Upper Court St., Binghamton, New York 13904, U.S.

July 1 — Dickson Motel, Fairview, Tennessee 37062, U.S.